Waltham Forest Libraries

Please return this item by the last date stamped. The loan may be
renewed unless required by another customer.

SEPT 2018		

D0754995

Need to renew your books?
http://www.walthamforest.gov.uk/libraries or
Dial 0333 370 4700 for Callpoint – our 24/7 automated telephone renewal
line. You will need your library card number and your PIN. If you do not
know your PIN, contact your local library.

To my dear, kind friend Ruth Washington.   A.B.

For my not so shy angels, Immie and
Elliot. From Mum, with love.   R.H.

Text copyright © 2018 Anne Booth
Illustrations copyright © 2018 Ruth Hearson
This edition copyright © 2018 Lion Hudson IP Limited

The right of Anne Booth to be identified as the author and of Ruth Hearson to be identified as
the illustrator of this work has been asserted by them in accordance with the Copyright, Designs and Patents Act 1988.

Published by Lion Children's Books
an imprint of
Lion Hudson Limited
Wilkinson House, Jordan Hill Business Park
Banbury Road, Oxford OX2 8DR, England
www.lionhudson.com/lionchildrens

Paperback ISBN 978 0 7459 7737 9

First edition 2018

A catalogue record for this book is available from the British Library

Printed and bound in China, May 2018, LH54

Anne Booth ★ Ruth Hearson

Jenny, the Shy Angel

LION
CHILDREN'S

Up in the sky at Christmastime
the angels like to sing,
and all around you see them
doing busy sorts of things.

Except for angel Jenny —
who is a little shy.
She likes to wait until the
other angels have gone by.

"Dear Jenny, come and fly with us,"
the other angels say,
"and celebrate the wonder and the joy of Christmas day."
"Come, sing a Christmas carol,
be happy in the crowd."

"Oh dear," says little Jenny.
"It's all a bit too loud."

"This time is truly wonderful,
hosannas fill the air.
I see the shepherds laugh and rush
to show how much they care.

"The other angels are so nice,
and all so very kind,
but when they rush and fly about
I'd rather stay behind."

"You go," she says, "I'll mind the sheep.
Go – run along now – hurry!
I'll stay and sing my praises here,
so no one has to worry."

So off the shepherds rush to see
the newborn King of Kings,
the Lord of Lords in Bethlehem:
the God of everything.

And Angel Jenny cuddles lambs
and hears a whispered tale –
of rain and rainbows, floods and arks
recounted by two snails.

Little mice take courage
and sit upon her wing,
to tell the tales that they have learnt,
of their creator-King.

Angel Jenny sees the world,
and all that God put there.
And in the quiet of the night
she says a little prayer.

"You know I love you, God," she prays.
"I want to praise you too,
but when there's lots of noise about
I don't know what to do."

"Oh, Angel Jenny!" cries an owl,
"please babysit for me:
I have to leave the little owls
to fly and get their tea."

So Jenny soars up to the tree,
and little feathered friends
have stories told, are sung to sleep
until the long night's end.

And in her arms owl babies doze,
while softly shines the moon.
And under stars the sheep sleep sound;
the morning comes too soon.

The shepherds thank her for her care,
the owls come back to sleep.

They tell her of the baby born:
"Go – have a little peep!"

So as the dawn turns night clouds pink
Angel Jenny flies
in through a special stable door
And sees...

in baby eyes:
the love that made the sun and stars;
that made the night and day;
who cares for lambs, mice, snails and owls,
and us in every way.

"I love you, Jesus," Jenny smiles
and cuddles in her arms,
the source of all the love there is,
protecting us from harm.

And as his tired mother sleeps
and Joseph takes his rest,
quiet Jenny knows that now
she has the job that's best.

Other Christmas titles from Lion Hudson

On That Christmas Night   *Lois Rock - Alison Jay*

Tales from Christmas Wood   *Suzy Senior - James Newman Gray*

The Animals' Christmas   *Elena Pasquali - Giuliano Ferri*

Countdown to Christmas   *Juliet David - Paul Nicholls*

The Midnight Visitors   *Juliet David - Jo Parry*

The Fox's Tale   *Nick Butterworth - Mick Inkpen*